THE BEST OF YOU

The Best of You

WINNING AUDITIONS YOUR WAY

Craig Wallace

OYSTER MINING COMPANY, INC

Published by Oyster Mining Company, Inc. Chicago, Illinois
E-mail: publishing@oystermining.com

This book may be purchased for educational, business,
or sales promotional use. For information please e-mail
publishing@oystermining.com
Attention: Special Markets Department.

Designed and typeset by Gopa & Ted2, Inc.
Author's Photograph by Brooke Blanchard
Edited by Melissa Culverwell

Library of Congress Control Number: 2006931907

ISBN-10: 0-9788362-0-0
ISBN-13: 978-0-9788362-0-7

10 9 8 7 6 5 4 3 2 1

▶Table of Contents

To Connie

Whose persistence and diligence started me on this path
—and whose love, belief, and generosity
turned it into a path with heart.

▶Acknowledgements

WHEN I DECIDED to write this book I was very clear about what I wanted to say. I was not nearly as clear, however, about how to *write* what I wanted to say. That was a problem.

First I turned to books. *Bird by Bird*, by Anne Lamott, *On Writing*, by Stephen King, and *The Spirit of Writing*, edited by Mark Robert Waldman were invaluable resources and wonderful companions.

Next, I sought the help of my friends, family, colleagues and students. I found among them the best teachers I could have asked for.

To all these people, my thanks, for the support and friendship they've shown me and my book:

To Kay Shute, Steven Schub, Kerry Madden, Dian Ohm, Constance Shute and David Boller who read early, rickety drafts of the manuscript and gave me wonderful notes, as well as sweet words of encouragement.

To Brad Lemack, Doug Warhit, Tim Morrell, Dana Shute, and all of the people who put up with my seemingly endless stream of questions—and were so generous and knowledgeable with their answers.

To Chris Murphy, Kristen Lowman, Mary Ambrose, Angela Brazil, Stephen Thorne, Susan Chenault, Sheri Gross, and Mary Anne Page for always being in my corner, and for filling it with so much warmth and laughter.

To Melissa Culverwell, who lifted the quality of this book from her first set of notes through her elegant and thoughtful editing.

To Dan Kagan—who understands me—which is a miracle—so is he—enough said.

To Jennifer Westaway who handled the thankless job of reading the very first draft of this book with amazing grace and tact. It is beyond my capabilities as a writer to express how much her intelligence, honesty and enthusiasm meant to this project—and mean to me.

And finally, to all of the students I am so honored to teach and from whom I never stop learning.

▶Introduction

A<small>N AUDITION</small> is an opportunity. It is a chance for you, the actor, to show a person or group of people who you are and what is uniquely yours to add to a role.

Yes, it is a process. It is not, however, rocket science. Actors (and many teachers) like to make auditioning seem harder than it is, which only serves to make the process more intimidating and nerve-wracking. This is the reason that most actors walk into an audition like they are going in front of a firing squad. They look at the audition as a necessary evil, the thing standing between them and the job. They feel they have no creative freedom and must do what they think the people in the room want to see. They shut down and leave their best qualities out of their reading, fearing those qualities will not be right for the role.

> ▶ *I'll let you in on a secret: the casting directors don't know what they are looking for until they see it.*

You are auditioning for television shows and films that have not yet been produced. Given that the audition is usually the first time the material has been read aloud, how many decisions could have been made? If the casting director and/or the producers had already decided on a specific direction the role was going to take, they would have called an actor whose work they were already familiar with and offered the part to him or her.

▶ *At this very early point in the casting process, the casting directors have no preconceived notions about the role. Neither should you!*

They are looking for possibilities: the unique and personal set of possibilities that are yours to offer.

I realize that freedom is not a word most actors would associate with an audition, but you really do have a great deal of freedom in this process.

Your audition technique needs to help you to access the qualities that you have to add to the role, give you a way to incorporate those qualities into the piece, and provide the technical means to present those qualities in a clear, strong, and compelling manner.

Your work should be done by the time you walk into the room. Most actors, however, are still working in the audition. They are using a technique that is more complicated and convoluted than it needs to be. They wind up showing us nothing but effort and process. People auditioning you, unfortunately, don't want to see your work and don't care about your process.

▶ *They simply want to see you.*

For that reason, your technique must be simple and straightforward. You need to be like athletes who train and train so that when they walk onto the court, field or track, they can relax the mind and body and simply perform—secure in the knowledge that their preparation will support them. When you watch these athletes you see no stress and no work. All you see is the effortless connection to themselves and their abilities.

I used to pass an antique store on my way to work many years ago. In the window were two mirrors, one worked, the other didn't. When you looked into the broken mirror all you saw were swirls of black and silver. It had lost the property of depth; all you could see were patterns and textures. The mirror next to it simply did what we expect mirrors to do: it reflected the depth of the image in front of it.

Many actors, when they are auditioning, are so focused on showing off their skills and selling their work that the truth of who they really are becomes as blurry as the image in the broken mirror.

The goal of the actor should be that of the reflective mirror: to present with honesty and simplicity the depth of who they are and what they have to offer the role.

Most actors choose to show textures primarily because they lack confidence in themselves. They feel that they need to *do* something in order to be noticed. They don't have a technique, a way of preparing, that allows them the confidence to audition with depth: *to simply be.*

The technique that follows is designed to give you that confidence. It will provide you with all the necessary tools and skills that will enable you to walk into any audition and show the people in the room who you are and what you have to add to the role with ease, power and fearlessness. It will help you tear down the walls of effort and stress that are built by insecurity and doubt— to remove the texture and reveal the depth.

Finally, the technique will provide you with the most important tool of all: the belief that what is uniquely yours to offer is all you need in order to breathe authentic, compelling life into any role you are auditioning for.

▶Part One

THE WALLACE AUDITION TECHNIQUE

▶The Three Decisions

THE PURPOSE of the audition is for you to show the specific possibilities that you, and only you, can bring to the role. In order to achieve this you need to make three key decisions about the role you will be reading for.

These decisions must bring out the qualities that most strongly represent your uniqueness and individuality. Each decision needs to represent your particular point of view. *It is essential that the people you are reading for are learning something about you every second that you are in the room.*

The decisions provide your unique framework for the piece.

What follows are three questions that will lead you to your decisions. At first glance, these questions may seem like simple common sense. In fact, they are. But there is a big difference between answering these questions in preparation for an *audition* as opposed to a *finished performance*: every answer that you give must be based on what you want the people in the room to learn about you; not the character, not the text, but you!

The answers to the following three questions provide the basis of this technique. In every audition piece, whatever the length or form (drama, sit-com, feature film, etc.), these questions need to be answered. The decisions that result from your answers will represent what is distinctly yours to bring to the role.

DECISION #1: WHAT IS YOUR INTENT?

The first step in preparing an audition piece is to read it through once and make your first decision by answering the question: *what is my intent for the character?*

In class, students always nod their heads when I say this, as if to tell me, "What else would I do? That's the way I approach every acting challenge." That is when I know that they haven't taken in the most important part of the question:

▶ *What is **my** intent for the character?*

Not the writer's intent, not the casting director's intent, but *my* intent.

What you are asking yourself in this first step is, "What do I want this person to want?"

Please note that I said to read the piece only once before you find your intent. The reason for this is that if you read the piece only once initially, you won't be as tempted to look to the text for your answers and you will be free to make *your own decisions* about the material. The more you read a piece before making your decisions about it, the harder it is to see past the writing and find your point of view.

It may be difficult at first to resist the temptation to read the piece over and over again. Just remember, you are preparing an audition, and the answers that will get you the job come from you.

Read the following sample piece through once.

When you have finished, you will be asked to identify your intent. Remember, it is *your* intent that we are looking for. Read the piece to get the sense of it. Do not depend on it for your answers!

Int: Living room of Beth and Bob's apartment. Beth is kneeling on the floor, surrounded by clothes, books, etc. She is packing.

Enter Bob.

Bob
Hi, sorry I'm late…what are you doing?

Beth
Exactly what it looks like. I'm packing up.

Bob
I can see that, would you care to tell me why? Beth, come on, talk to me.

Beth
I was planning on talking to you when we had lunch today, which was four hours ago, in case you lost your watch.

Bob
Alright, alright, look, I'm sorry. I was stuck at the hospital. An intern doesn't exactly get to come and go as he pleases. We'll have dinner and talk this out.

Beth
And during dinner you'll probably be paged, and Nancy will order you back to the hospital. No thanks Bob, I've had enough.

Bob
Beth, this is what I do, and Nancy is my supervisor. You knew all of this when we moved in together, but lately all you do is complain. It's like you think I actually want to be away from you.

Beth
Marcy says that Dan doesn't work half the hours you do and you guys are in the same internship. What am I supposed to think? All of your energy goes to your patients, and to your beautiful, perky supervisor. There's nothing left for me! God, it's like living with my father again.

Bob
Don't compare me to your father. Look, I know how he treated your mother. I know he ignored her, talked down to her and worse, but that's not who I am.

Beth
That's the problem, Bob, I don't know who you are anymore.

Bob
(exiting)
Honey, I'm too tired for this right now. Stay if you want, leave if you want. I'm going back to the hospital.

Most actors would look at this piece and say, "The intent of these characters is so obvious: Beth wants to leave and Bob wants her to stay." That is what the text may be dictating.

► *But what about* you? *What intent really interests* you?

> ► **SAMPLE INTENTS FOR BETH:** To get Bob to tell me he loves me, to find out if he is having an affair, to run away from the memory of my father, to gain comfort from Bob, to convince Bob he should quit medicine.

> ► **SAMPLE INTENTS FOR BOB:** To get Beth to stay, to let her know that I care, to use this chance to leave her, to tell her about my affair with Nancy, to convince her she is making a huge mistake.

Use the space below to write down your *intent for whichever charac-ter applies to you: Beth or Bob.*

As you can see, there are as many different intents as there are different people reading the piece. Your job is to not stop until you find the one that drives *you* through the piece with the highest degree of energy and passion.

Answering the question "What is my intent?" with honesty and clarity will ensure, right from the get-go, that the piece has meaning to you. You will have resisted the temptation to have your reading be just a recitation of the words on the page.

> ▶ *Remember, if your intent is compelling and interesting for you to achieve, it will be equally compelling and interesting to watch.*

It is the first step in making the role a representation of who you are and what is uniquely yours to offer.

DECISION #2: WHAT IS YOUR RELATIONSHIP?

After you have decided on your intent, you need to take a look at the relationships in the piece. That includes not only the person you are talking to, but also the people you are talking about.

How do you *feel* about the other person/people in the scene? What are the relationships that have the most resonance for you?

It may help at this point to take a moment and look at the feelings that exist behind the meaningful relationships in your own life. This can be a very valuable exercise to do because, just like the decision of intent, the decisions you make regarding the relationships in the piece need to be connected and compelling to you.

So, let's go back to the sample piece on the previous page. Again, resist the temptation to settle for the obvious. Find the relationships that are the most powerful ones for you.

Note that there are other relationships in the piece. There is Beth and Bob's relationship to Nancy, their relationship to Beth's father, to Marcy and Dan, and to Bob's job.

All of these relationships—the person/people that you are talking to, and the people/situations that you are talking about—must be defined from your perspective.

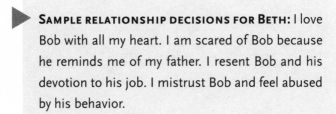

SAMPLE RELATIONSHIP DECISIONS FOR BETH: I love Bob with all my heart. I am scared of Bob because he reminds me of my father. I resent Bob and his devotion to his job. I mistrust Bob and feel abused by his behavior.

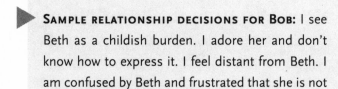

SAMPLE RELATIONSHIP DECISIONS FOR BOB: I see Beth as a childish burden. I adore her and don't know how to express it. I feel distant from Beth. I am confused by Beth and frustrated that she is not the woman I fell in love with.

Use the space below to establish and write down your relationship decisions for either Beth or Bob.

Don't stop until you find the relationships that mean something to you, the relationships that will offer us a window into your personality.

Finding the relationships that enhance your point of view on the material will go a long way toward breaking you out of the pack.

Most actors don't adequately consider the relationships in the piece. They take the relationship at face value and don't go the extra step of considering how they feel about the other person or people.

▶ *They are working under the misconception that the audition is all about their lines and their lines only.*

There is at least one other person in the scene. They aren't going anywhere, so stop trying to ignore them! Decide who they are and how you feel about them. The added dimension that this decision will bring to your auditions is invaluable.

I was recently in a casting session that illustrated the importance of establishing strong relationships. The show was a pilot about four kids starting their freshman year in college. One of the series regular roles being cast was that of the guidance counselor. The actors reading for this part had a huge challenge. There were 12 pages of material in which the guidance counselor had only four lines! There were no cuts in the piece, so the actors auditioning for this role had page after page with no lines at all.

Keep in mind, the producers didn't do this to be mean. They had a very specific reason. The role of the guidance counselor was primarily going to be a sounding board for the students. He would be the one to whom the students would tell their hopes, dreams, fears and secrets. So the producers knew they needed an actor who had extraordinary listening skills and could convey almost all of his thoughts and feelings through his eyes.

We saw eight actors for the role that day. Most of them were not up to the challenge. In general, they were uncomfortable during the long stretches where they had no lines. Some of them became fidgety and nervous and most went a bit dead behind the eyes. You could tell that they didn't have any relationship to the characters they were listening to and were just marking time until their next line.

One actor, however, was more than up to the task. He was fascinating to watch. During the long passages in the text where he had no lines, his eyes were so alive that you swore he was speaking. He had done what the other actors had neglected to do. He had made strong and meaningful decisions about the relationships in the piece. Watching him, you knew exactly how he felt about each person. His reactions were entirely different depending on which character was speaking to him, and you could see the passion he had for his job as a counselor. He was so dynamic when he was listening that he didn't even need the few lines that he had!

In this case, the relationship decisions were all these actors had to break themselves out of the pack. The few lines that they had to read certainly weren't going to do it. One actor understood this. His reward was the role.

DECISION #3: WHAT ARE YOUR CHOICES?

A choice is a quality of yours that will bring each line of the piece to life. Choices need to be active and honest.

The decisions that you make regarding your choices for the piece are your chance to show the people in the room what you want them to know about you. Each choice should represent a specific part of your particular personality.

You will be hired based on what you have to add to the piece, not how well you spit back what is already there on the page. Your choices are those additions.

For your reference, here are some examples of active, playable choices. Of course there are many others, but hopefully this short list will help guide you toward the choices that are truly yours.

ANGRY	ANXIOUS	COCKY	BITTER
FIRM	CAUTIOUS	JEALOUS	CYNICAL
CALM	INTENSE	PASSIONATE	HURT
ARROGANT	HYSTERICAL	EDGY	SEDUCTIVE
VICIOUS	FLIRTATIOUS	PANICKED	JOYFUL
NONCHALANT	HAPPY	DIRECT	SHY
SAD	GENTLE	DISMISSIVE	STERN
SYMPATHETIC	WARM	LUSTFUL	DESPERATE

The choices that you make are a reflection of your experience, not anyone else's. The choices are also what you are going to use to achieve what you have decided you want (intent), and will also be specific to how you feel toward the person(s) you are talking to or about (relationship).

▶ **POSSIBLE DECISIONS FOR BETH:**

SAMPLE INTENT: To convince Bob that I am more important than his career.

SAMPLE RELATIONSHIP: I feel both hurt and afraid of him.

Now you need to ask yourself how you would convince someone who has hurt you and that you fear that you are an important, valuable person.

SAMPLE CHOICES: Cautious, desperate, nervous, angry, proud, sad, bitter, vulnerable.

▶ **POSSIBLE DECISIONS FOR BOB:**

SAMPLE INTENT: To convince Beth that my career is important to both of our futures.

SAMPLE RELATIONSHIP: I love her but resent her neediness.

So, ask yourself how you would convince someone who is important to you, but is driving you a little nuts, that spending so much time at work is good for both of you.

SAMPLE CHOICES: Frustrated, mean, warm, sarcastic, dismissive, firm, defensive.

Use the space below to write down your choices for either Beth or Bob.

Actors ask me all the time, "What if my choices aren't the ones the casting director is looking for?" My response is always the same: "They don't know what they are looking for until you show it to them." Any choices you make that you are connected to will tell them something about you and what you have to add to the role. That is exactly what they are looking for!

Be very careful that the choices that you make are honestly yours to make. Make the choices that you believe are the best. Don't try to second-guess what the casting director wants to see. This will only tempt you to make choices that you feel will please them.

Believe me, they will not be pleased. All they will end up seeing is you disconnecting and selling out.

No matter what type of material you are given—drama, comedy, good writing, or mediocre writing—*your choices should be so strong that your individual and unique personality will shine through and be felt by everyone in the audition.*

Answering the questions of what your intent, relationship and choices are, honestly and personally, will bring the words on the page to life. If we can see who that character is through your eyes and your experience, you will have put yourself in a great position to get the job.

▶The Technical Aspect

You HAVE MADE DECISIONS of intent, relationship and choices that are strong, true indications of who you are and what you have to offer the role.

Now, you must make sure that those decisions are delivered in the clearest, cleanest way possible.

As wonderful as your work may be so far, it won't mean much if the way you deliver it is muddy and unfocused.

That said, I want to be very clear that good technique is not, in and of itself, enough. It is a part of the process and exists to support the decisions that you have already made. Many actors will get an audition piece and immediately "break it down" technically before they have established what they want to do with it.

This results in just a reading of the material and will give us no answers about you—other than the fact that you can read.

BEATS

You may not know it, but you have already broken the piece down into beats. For the purpose of an audition, each choice that you have made is a separate beat.

Example: If your choice for your first three lines of the piece is anger, that is your first beat. If your choice for your next four lines is sarcasm, that is your second beat, and so on through the piece.

As you decide what choices are yours to offer, and exactly where each one has the highest resonance in the text, the piece becomes more and more a reflection of your vision. You are no longer in danger of being one of the herd who is satisfied with simply reciting the piece as written.

EYES UP

There are four times during an audition piece when you will use these beats to help you be comfortably off of the page and engaged with the reader. I call this being "eyes up."

Number One: Opening Beat

The first time you are going to be eyes up is on your opening beat (your first choice). The first impression that you make during the piece needs to be strong, direct and clear. If the other character has the first line or lines in the piece, make sure that you are eyes up and listening. We need to see right off the bat that you are an attentive and solid listener (more on that later). You may either stay eyes up and respond with your opening-beat or go down to the page, get the beat, and come back up to deliver it. The choice is yours.

Number Two: Payoff Lines

Within each beat, there will be a line or group of words (meaning it doesn't have to be a full sentence) that expresses your choice the most clearly. These are called *payoff lines*. They are the lines that convey the meaning of the choice in the strongest way for you.

Example: You have made a choice of anger for three lines of the piece. This is now one of your beats. Let's say the lines are: "I don't like you very much." "I think that you are funny-looking and obnoxious." "I am going to stab you in the heart." Now, if it were me, the line that would express the choice of anger the strongest is "I am going to stab you in the heart." That is my payoff line. So when that line comes up in the beat I would be eyes up.

Why is this important? *You have identified the payoff lines as being the strongest lines in the piece for you. You don't want us to miss them.* They provide the biggest key into your personality and point of view. So eyes up and no cheating! What I mean by that is, you should be up during the entire payoff line, not sliding up at the beginning and sneaking down before you have finished delivering it. You need to make sure that the impact of these lines is not watered down.

Number Three: Closing Beat

Just as being eyes up and engaged is important on your opening beat, so it is on your closing beat. You need to end the piece as strongly as you started it. So, your closing beat is always eyes up and to the reader. Your last impression must be equally as powerful as your first.

Number Four: Listening

The other time you are to be eyes up during your reading may seem obvious, but it is the one that most actors miss in the audition: when the other person is talking. This is also known as *listening*. No worse thing could be said about an actor than "They don't listen." Yet it is exactly what casting directors find themselves saying about almost every actor they see. I have heard so many excuses over the years from actors as to why they don't listen in an audition, and yet it is the most important thing you can do. For example, actors will say, "Well, if I'm listening, I won't get back down to the page in time for my next line." In time? Who is timing you? The line is not going to run off the page just because you're not staring at it.

▶ *You are not just talking in an audition, **you are responding**.*

In order to respond with freshness and spontaneity, you need to be really and truly hearing what is being said to you. When you are listening, you are connecting to the other person, and since you have fleshed out the relationship, you know what that person means to you.

▶ *Listening is your chance to show us the meaning*
  of that relationship.

It is your chance to show us exactly how you feel about the other person in the scene.

Listening is the one opportunity to let the people auditioning you see who you are and what you have to offer without the encumbrance of the lines—lines that they have been hearing all day long. It is the purest hit they are going to get on you. Don't give it away!

EYES DOWN

Defining the beats of the piece based on your choices will also help you establish when it is most effective for you to have your eyes down on the page.

You may be asking at this point, "If my eyes are up for my opening and closing beats, for my payoff lines, and when I'm listening, where are they the rest of the time?" Down on the page, that's where. Don't freak out!

I know that this may seem counterintuitive at first. Many actors are taught that one of the first and most important things to do in preparing to perform is to memorize the lines and be off book. But, remember: an audition is not a performance; it is not a finished product.

▶ *You are reading for the role, not performing it.*

If your audition looks like it is a finished performance, it will be assumed that what you have just shown is all that you have to offer, and you will not be asked to make adjustments or changes. It will be left at that. The short periods of time you are down on the page are totally appropriate to an audition.

When you think of it, if you are eyes up on your opening and closing beats, your payoff lines, and the other person's lines, you're not down that much anyway, so don't worry that the connection will be lost. The times that you have chosen to be down on the page give the people in the room the opportunity to take a look at you, and really see you. If you are always eyes up, they lose that opportunity because you are in their faces the entire time. It is the job of the casting director to really watch you and take you in, not be your scene partner. The times that you are down on the page give them the chance to do that.

If your relationship is strong, the connection will not be broken by a moment down on the page. Also, the next time that you are eyes up during the piece will be even stronger and more effective.

▶ *All audition pieces are ultimately conversations between two or more people.*

Most of us don't stare at the person or people we're talking with during an entire conversation—neither should you in the audition!

PUTTING IT TOGETHER

Now, let's go back to Beth and Bob. Apply the technique you've learned to the choices you have made. Identify your opening and closing beats, find your payoff lines (underline them if you need to), commit to the relationship you have worked out so that listening is effortless and natural, and run the piece once or twice to get the feeling of this technique.

You will notice that it takes a fraction of a second every time you bring your eyes up and down. That is a good thing! Those fractions of seconds help to guard against the number one enemy of actors in auditions: *going too fast*. Let's face it: the entire audition process is set up for you to go too fast. There are 40 actors waiting, the session is running late, the casting director or reader is reading very quickly, and you have adrenaline pumping. If you don't have a technique that ensures that, no matter what the circumstances, you will go at your own pace—you will be out of the room before you even realize you were in it.

All of your technical decisions are based on the decisions that you have made about the material. If you commit to the technical aspect, you can be totally confident that the piece will be delivered at your pace and in your rhythm.

If you have not worked the material through technically, you will try to match the rhythm of the casting director, which will invariably be too fast to convey what you want to show them. But, if you have taken care of the technical aspect of your audition, you will set the pace and the casting director will follow your lead.

You will now be the one running the session. They can relax and watch all of the wonderful possibilities that you are putting forth. This will also help give them the confidence they need to give you the job. You are showing them a complete package, and you are making every second count.

► *How you are reading the piece will be telling them just as much about you as the decisions you have brought to it.*

FINDING YOUR TECHNIQUE

Now that you have read and applied the three decisions and the technical work to the sample piece, you may have found that certain steps in the technique as a whole warrant more of your attention than others. For instance, finding an interesting intent may be easier for you than identifying the most compelling choices; or the technical eyes up, eyes down work may be a cinch, but discovering the relationship that has the most meaning for you takes more time. That is absolutely fine!

I think it is a contradiction to say that each person is different and unique, and in the same breath say that there is somehow one exact way for each person to prepare.

The degree of focus and amount of time you spend on each step of this technique will depend on, among other factors, your prior training, the unique way that you process information, and your life experience.

▶ *The goal in an audition is not to present a technique, it is to use your technique in such a way that it frees you to show the people in the room who you are.*

The Wallace Audition Technique is a flexible framework. Your job is to bend the framework to suit your specific needs as a person and as an actor—in other words, to make it your own.

▶Exploring and Experimenting:

An Exercise for Finding Your Strongest Choices

A COMMON PROBLEM shared by many actors is that once they have made their choices, they don't really go for them. They lack the confidence it takes to totally commit.

When this happens in class I ask the actor how they feel about their choices. They usually respond, "They were okay." Ugh! "Okay" will not get you jobs. When I get to the bottom of what they mean by "okay," I find out that they do feel that the choices they made have relevance to who they are and what they have to offer. However, they have a nagging feeling that there might be better and stronger choices they could have made. Their problem is they don't know how to find them.

When I ask what they do about this, they say they think about other choices they could make. They read the piece again, think some more, read the piece once again, think...and on and on.

Has it occurred to you yet that the main problem is the amount of *thinking* going on?

Your brain is not the place to look if you want to access who you are.

▶ *Your brain will only tell you the most logical choice to make, not necessarily the most interesting choice.*

The brain's function is to make sense of things, put things in order, and edit out anything that isn't logical.

While these functions of the brain have their value, they are extremely limiting in any creative pursuit, auditioning included. The most interesting choices that you can make come from your gut, not from your brain.

Here is an exercise that will relax the editing powers of the brain. It will help you find choices where they really live inside of you and it will give you a fun way to explore them as fully as possible. After doing this exercise, you will never want to be without it. It will become an invaluable part of your audition process.

Exercise:

Let's return to our old pals Bob and Beth. By this time, you have made your decision of intent. You have made the relationships sing with meaning for you and you have made the choices that you feel will say the most about you.

Now, put those decisions aside.

Pick the piece up and do the first thing that comes to you. It can be anything you *feel* like doing. Use the mood you're in. Do something really fun or off the wall. Go ahead, nobody can see! Whatever it is that you choose, do that one thing 100%, all the way through the piece, every line, every word, every breath, just that one choice.

Now choose another emotion, anything you want. Some of my students find it fun to choose the opposite of the first choice. For example, if they chose panic the first time through, they might choose calm for the second. Whatever gets the creative juices flowing and is fun for you to do, go ahead!

The reason each choice is done one at a time and done 100% is to relax the power the brain normally has over you. It may not make sense to use the choice of panic. But if you do it anyway, the brain will start to get out of your way. It will see that its power to tell you what to do is weakening and it will release much of its control. When this happens, you become free to explore and find the choices that feel the best for you. *Remember, the choices that feel the best to you are the ones that are going to say the most about you.*

Do the piece as many different ways as you want. No thinking, just doing. Stop when you have explored every choice that you feel you want to explore.

Write down the choices you explored in this space.

Now, go back and take a look at the choices you made for Beth or Bob before doing this exercise. See which ones you want to keep and which ones you may want to change based on what you discovered by doing the exercise. Make the changes that strengthen the piece for you and add the choices that you discovered during the exercise that truly speak to who you are.

You will find that the piece is much richer than it was before you did this exploring. Even the choices you didn't change will take on the color and dimension of the different emotions that you examined.

When my students do this exercise for the first time, they almost always say, "I can't believe some of the choices I discovered. I never would have thought of them if I hadn't done this exercise!" That is exactly the point.

▶ *They wouldn't have have* **thought** *of them, they had to* **do** *them in order to find the ones they were truly connected to.*

You will now know that you are walking into the audition with exactly the choices that say the most about you. Not because you thought about them, but because you did them.

You will commit to your choices with the certainty that comes from knowing that you are doing exactly what is right for you to be doing.

And finally, I promise you that Bob and Beth are now a lot more interesting than they were before you applied this exercise to the piece. And you know why they're more interesting? Because you have discovered the choices that are the most interesting for you to bring to them!

▶Adjustments

BEING ASKED to make an adjustment is a wonderful thing. It means that you have connected to your intent, relationship, and choices in á way that has made the people auditioning you want to see more. Adjustments are not difficult. However, they can be tricky if you are unclear as to what is expected of you. Listed below are the three things the casting director and/or producers are looking for in an adjusted reading:

1) Do you understand what the adjustment means?

2) Are you able to deliver it?

3) Can you incorporate it into your initial reading?

We will go into more detail on the first two points in a moment.

First, I would like to address #3, the issue of incorporation. It is the one step that seems to trip actors up the most and cost them jobs.

Let's say that you have been asked to do your piece again and adjust it by being angrier.

Most actors then proceed to scream and yell during the entire adjusted reading, with no thought to what they did in the first reading.

The casting directors and/or producers are not looking to see if you can simply spit back the meaning of the word that they have given you. They are looking to see how that adjustment affects the choices that you brought into the room to begin with.

The word "adjustment" implies that something is being adjusted. What is being adjusted are the choices that you made and delivered in your initial reading.

> ▶ *It is an adjustment, not an overhaul. If they wanted to see an overhaul they would have asked for it. The fact that they use the word adjustment is not an accident.*

As I said earlier, you are still in the room because they liked what they saw. They want to continue to see the choices that they liked in the first place. They just want to see *if you are able to shift those choices in the direction of the adjustment.*

More on how to achieve that shift a little later. For now, let's take you through the three steps that will guide you effortlessly through this sometimes bumpy terrain.

You have finished your initial reading. The casting director says, "That was very good, now could you do it again, this time with more anger?"

1) **Take a deep breath**. You've done well! Any dynamic of "me against them" is gone. They have responded well to what you have shown them and they are on your side, so relax and remember to breathe. There is a shift coming up and you want your mind to be as clear as possible.

2) **Ask questions if you have them**. You don't want to get this far and blow it because you have a different definition of a word than they do. Also, casting directors will often speak in a shorthand that means something to them but may mean nothing to you. Phrase your questions in a way that will get you the most information possible.

   A good way to ask a question might be: "Is there a specific way you'd like the anger delivered?"

If there is, they will tell you. You may, however, get the standard casting director response, which is: "Show me what you would like to do." All that means is that they want to see how the adjustment affects your initial work. Either way, you will be as clear as possible about what they expect out of the adjustment.

3) **When you are sure you know exactly what the adjustment is, ask for a moment.** You will need a few seconds to incorporate the adjustment.

If you have prepared the piece using the Wallace Audition Technique, you have a fast and easy way to do this.

Remember your payoff lines? You'd better! That is where you are going to put the adjustment. You have already identified them as being the strongest lines of each beat, so if you put the adjustment on these lines, you can be sure it will be seen. Take the moment that you have asked for to scan the piece quickly. Identify your payoff lines again and make the adjustment the new choice for each of those lines.

What about the rest of the lines? Keep them the same as they were when you first did the piece. You will find that, without any effort, they will shift slightly toward the meaning of the adjustment.

So, the adjustment is anger. Let's say that your first payoff line is the fourth line in the piece. You know anger will be seen on that fourth line. However, without you trying to do anything differently, the first three lines of the piece will make the slight shift toward anger. Those lines will have just a bit more edge to them because you are now working toward anger. And because you haven't consciously changed them, they will also retain the integrity of your initial choice.

That is the balancing act of adjustments: shifting the meaning of your initial choice *slightly,* not throwing it out. So many actors buy into the temptation of overdoing the adjustment. They are much too willing to throw all of their original work out in an effort to perform the adjustment, to please the casting director.

Doing so is not pleasing. All it does is show a lack of confidence in yourself—a feeling that the casting director will undoubtedly share.

▶ *Look at an adjustment as you would a piece of direction.*

In fact, one of the main reasons adjustments are given is to see if you can take direction. If you were on a set and the director said to you after a take, "That was fine, but on the next take I'd like to see you angrier," you wouldn't scream and yell all the way through the next take. You would take some time and figure out where the anger would work best in the scene. Well, that is what you should do in an audition. The only difference is that you are making the adjustment work for you by using your payoff lines.

Before we finish this topic, here are a couple of side notes that will ensure you are able to compete with the best.

When you are adjusted, it is very rare that you will be allowed to get through the entire piece again. Usually, all you have the chance to read is a couple of beats. So, if you have a longer piece (in the world of auditioning, anything over a page is considered long), make sure to pay special attention to the first two or three payoff lines. They're probably all you'll get to work with.

Finally, don't forget how important your listening is! The adjustment needs to show up in more than just the lines. The way that you listen and react will shift as well. Be sure that the casting director can see that. Resist the urge to race to your payoff lines. *Remember, the shift toward the adjustment will be occurring through-out the piece, including (and especially) when you are listening.*

To review: Relax, breathe, ask questions if you have them, take a moment to re-identify your payoff lines, put the adjustment on the payoff lines, tell the reader you are ready, open your mouth, open your ears—and all will be well.

►Nerves

THE WALLACE AUDITION TECHNIQUE is designed to give you an effective way of preparing for your auditions. It is also here to help you deal with problems that may be holding you back from the career you want to have. So in this chapter, we will be discussing how you can use this technique to overcome one of the biggest roadblocks to success: nerves.

"I get so nervous in my auditions, how do I relax and keep nerves from getting in my way?" Does this sound familiar? It is the question that I am asked more than any other.

In order to address nerves, we first need to look at their cause. There is a psychological paradigm that deals with this. It is a remarkably simple formula that contains three elements: doubt, fear and anxiety. By definition, the last element of a paradigm can't exist without the elements that go before. So, if we see how we can remove doubt from the equation, the anxiety or nervousness will have no reason to exist.

The following are some examples of situations that create doubt in the audition process:

1) I am not good enough.

2) I am not right for the role.

3) I don't think my choices are strong enough.

4) That person in the waiting room looks better for the part than me.

5) They'll probably go for a name.

6) I am nervous and I shouldn't be.

7) I have to be perfect.

Any one of these doubts can provoke nervousness, and when you are experiencing two or three of them at a time it can become crippling.

Let's address each point on the above list by looking at the reality of the situation—without the emotional baggage.

1) You are as good, if not better, than anyone else auditioning for the role. Each actor is different and has a variety of possibilities to offer the part. Your job is simply to offer yours and not worry about theirs.

2) The very fact that there is a casting session taking place means that the casting director and/or producers don't know exactly what they are looking for. They don't know what "right" means for the role yet. If they did, they would have called the actors they knew were "right" and hired them over the phone. So at this point there is no reason for you to be anxious about being "wrong." *You can't be "wrong" if what is "right" has yet to be established.*

3) If you made choices that are compelling and an honest representation of who you are—if they reflect your point of view on the material; if you stay committed to them and to yourself—then they are strong enough. So look at your choices. If they do all of those things, there is no reason to doubt them, or to doubt yourself.

4) The other people in the waiting room are there because the casting people want to see a range of possibilities for the role. No decisions have been made. No one person has an advantage before they have read. As I've noted above, if one actor was absolutely "right" for the role, they would have been offered the role and there would be no casting session. The fact that there is a casting session means the playing field is wide open and your chances are as good as anyone else's.

5) Yes, the casting directors/producers may decide to go for a name, or they may not. You have no control over that decision. What you *do* have control over is being so strong and committed in the room that they are left with no choice but to consider you. When you put your focus on what you can control and let the rest go, the doubt and anxiety will also be released.

6) The most detrimental way to deal with nerves is to fight them. A surefire way to make yourself even more nervous is to say, "I will not be nervous" or "I shouldn't be nervous." You are walking into a strange room full of people you don't know. It is perfectly natural, no matter how well prepared you are, to be a bit nervous.

Instead of fighting your nerves, why not simply say, "Yes, I am a little nervous." Nerves gain power over you when they are denied and/or fought against. They also calm down and fade away when they are honestly acknowledged. It is like a baby who is screaming to get attention. If you ignore him, or shout at him to stop, he will scream even louder. But if you pick the baby up and hold him for a minute he will quiet down. If you treat your nerves this way, they will not interfere with your work. In fact, they will work in your favor, adding extra energy and life to your reading.

7) Perfection is not the goal in an audition. The goal is to show the people in the room what you have to add to the words on the page. You are a human being, auditioning to play another human being. *You are not a machine and not expected to behave as such.* Striving for perfection will cause huge amounts of doubt, fear, and anxiety for the simple reason that it is impossible to attain. You will always fall short no matter how hard you try. Remember what the real goal is: to show the parts of your humanity that will most effectively bring the character to life. And as I'm sure you know, humanity has very little to do with perfection.

So, when you become nervous before an audition, take a close look at the cause. You will find that the doubts and fears contained in the first list will give way quickly and easily to the gentle reason and humane logic of the second list.

►Part Two

CASE STUDIES

Now that you have learned the basics of The Wallace Audition Technique, reviewing case studies from class will help you see how this technique can help alleviate any specific problems that you may have.

All of these cases are based on students I have worked with in class. I chose them because the obstacles they were facing seem to be the ones faced by the greatest number of actors.

After each case, I will ask you how you would go about solving their particular problem. Consider each step of the technique as you know it thus far. The answers are there.

Remember, we keep this technique simple because we want to see *you* in the audition, not your technique. We also keep it simple so that if you are having a hard time with a piece of material, your answers will be equally simple to find.

When you have written down your answer to each of the following actors' dilemmas, turn the page and see how we worked it out in class. I bet we won't be far apart!

▶Case Study #1: David

D AVID WAS a young actor who had recently completed a master's program in theater. After graduation, he obtained an agent. When he joined my class, he had been sent out on about eight auditions. He got three callbacks and felt that he had done "a good job" with all of his auditions. He didn't understand why he wasn't getting more callbacks and booking the jobs he had been called back for. He had a wonderful personality, very funny, quick, and also quite bright.

The first piece I gave him was a scene between an obnoxious young cop and his superior. I asked him to identify his intent, define the relationship and make his choices. He had about 15 minutes to do so.

When he got up to do the piece, he was good in the sense that he read the material well and said he had a grasp on "the character."

However, the reading he gave was not representative of the person who I saw as so funny, clever and bright. He was just another actor reading a set of sides in a relatively professional way.

▶ *What do you think David's main problem was?*

What we discovered in class was that David had made the choices that he felt were right for the material—choices that were not, however, right for *him*.

His extensive theater training had taught him that all of his answers lay in the material.

He did not feel that what he had to offer the role was as important as making sense out of the text. So the choices that he came up with were flat and generic and showed us none of his uniqueness and energy.

He was overly concerned with "the character." Instead of showing us what qualities he had that would bring this young cop to life, he wound up showing us his opinion of what a brash young cop was.

My first question to David when he finished his reading was, "Where were *you?*

"I don't care about how you think the words on the page should sound, or who you think the character is. I care about what you have to add to the words you are reading, who the character is *through you.*"

I asked David what he would do in a similar situation. I knew, of course, that he had never been a cop, but he told me that there had been situations in his life where he had resorted to obnoxious or pushy behavior to prove his worthiness to someone he looked up to: perhaps his father, older brother, or boss.

I sent him out of the room to consider the choices that were his to make. When he read the piece again he was able to show me how he would go about proving himself to this other person. His choices were much more fun, energetic and clever than the choices he made for the first reading. He allowed me to see what he had to offer the role, not what he thought of the role.

Depending on the material for answers instead of finding them within yourself is a common issue for actors with an extensive theater background. The training in these programs is almost exclusively geared toward presenting a finished product. This is fine for performance. But as David learned, his job in the audition was not to perform the role of the cop. His job was to make the choices that would show us who the cop was through his eyes.

David learned a valuable lesson: auditioning requires different skills than performance.

►Case Study #2: Wendy

WENDY CAME TO ME in a panic. She had been acting professionally for about 5 years. Early in her career she enjoyed a good deal of success. Auditions were not a problem and she was able to make the decisions that worked well for her. The casting directors and producers were always clear as to what she had to add to the roles she was reading for. She was called back about 80% of the time and booked about half of those jobs. So far, so good.

However, in the year or so before I met her, her callback ratio had dropped considerably and she hadn't booked anything.

She was frustrated and said she felt disconnected. She was starting to "push" in her auditions. She said that she was afraid she had lost her talent.

▶ **What do you think Wendy's main problem was?**

I had a fairly strong feeling about what was happening to Wendy the first time I saw her work in class. It is a common phenomenon for many actors over the course of a career.

She was trying to connect to choices that no longer had the resonance for her that they once did.

She had grown and changed as a person and needed to find the choices that she could connect to at this point in her life. Instead of exploring any new choices, she continued to struggle to connect to the choices that had gotten her work in the past.

Wendy had not lost her talent, as she had feared. She had simply grown and needed to discover the choices that would tell the casting directors what she had to offer the roles *now*, not 5 years ago.

With patient exploration of the intents, relationships, and choices that had meaning to her now, she found new choices to bring to the material that wouldn't even have occurred to her a year earlier. She was no longer struggling to connect to who she *was*, but was able to show who she *is*. Her callback ratio rose back up and she began booking on a regular basis again.

Human beings are fluid creatures, constantly changing and growing. Like Wendy, you must check in with yourself on a regular basis to ensure that you are connecting with the choices that represent what you have to offer in the present moment. Your work must be bold, compelling and connected to the life you are living now!

▶Case Study #3: Joe

JOE WAS A WONDERFUL STUDENT. He was a very good actor and was truly dedicated to being better at auditioning and making a strong impression in the room.

He took very quickly to the idea of how important the decisions of intent and choices were to establishing his presence in a piece. He spent a lot of time deciding what he wanted the casting directors to know about him and made his choices accordingly. He was also good at identifying intents that would bring out these strong choices. Because of this, his work had energy and purpose and he was usually clear and committed to his decisions.

As honest and strong as his work was, something wasn't quite right. I always had the feeling that I had to look too hard to see exactly what he was offering. I had to make too much of an effort to connect with him.

▶ *Can you identify the missing component in Joe's work?*

Joe was not focusing on the decision of relationship nearly as much as he was the decisions of intent and choices.

His choices were connecting him to himself, and his intents were connecting him to the material. But, because his decisions about the relationships in the piece were not as strong, he was not connecting to me.

His work was not being delivered with any *outward focus*. He hadn't explored how he felt about the other person/people in the scene with enough depth to make them compelling to him. Therefore, his ability to listen and react with intensity and focus was severely diminished.

This was why I had the feeling that I had to look too hard to see what he was doing.

I worked with Joe to help him to identify relationships that had real meaning to him. We discussed various people in his life who were important to him and why. Through this exploration of the feelings behind those relationships, both good and bad, he was able to make stronger and more meaningful decisions.

His relationships became as interesting and true as his intent and choices. His auditions now had an even stronger point of view because he was delivering his choices to a person who had a specific meaning to him. The strength of his relationships ensured that all of his wonderful qualities were focused out toward the other person. He was now as connected to the reader as he was to himself.

Joe has gone on to have a wonderful career. The one thing that I always hear from casting directors is how present and involved he is when he is auditioning. That is a testament to the connection that is established when you make decisions about relationships that are compelling and meaningful to you.

▶Case Study #4: Joyce

JOYCE HAD A GOOD CAREER going when she joined class. Her main concern was consistency. Some of her auditions went great. She was relaxed and confident and would usually book the job or at least get a callback. She told me that in those auditions she would feel in sync with the words on the page and would, as she put it, "flow through the piece."

However, there were other auditions when she felt as if she was fighting the text. The piece would be written in a way that made the words come out sounding stiff and stilted. She would also have to fight the temptation to race through the material, which is understandable when you are uncomfortable with the words.

Joyce knew from experience that she would probably get just as many, if not more, of the pieces that made her feel stiff and awkward as she would the ones where she felt fluid and natural.

She knew there was something missing in her preparation, something that would allow her to "flow through" not just some, but all the pieces she auditioned with.

▶ *How would you help Joyce?*

Joyce's problem was a technical one. She was working the material line-to-line, not choice-to-choice. She wasn't breaking the piece into beats based on her choices. She was counting on the writing to establish her rhythm. She was unclear when to be eyes up and when to be eyes down on the page.

When she learned that it was her choices that established the beats, and that each beat had a payoff line that expressed her choice in the strongest way, she started to get on track.

The awkwardness she felt started to disappear as she technically worked through the material.

Each piece was now being delivered in her rhythm, and the temptation to rush went away.

Joyce realized that she was in control and was not a victim of the writing. By making strong choices, committing to being off the page on her payoff lines, and taking the time to listen, she was able to "flow through" every piece. The consistency that she knew she needed was now hers in every piece and in every audition.

►Case Study #5: Carl

CARL WAS A WONDERFUL STUDENT of mine who had been acting professionally for about 3 years after graduating from a college acting program. He came to class because his callback ratio was only about 30%. He was frustrated and felt that he was inconsistent in his auditions.

His work in class was generally solid and his instincts as to which choices were the strongest for him were usually right on.

There was, however, one problem. There were times when his work felt disjointed. He would show anger and then sadness and then sarcasm and then panic. But I would get the feeling that I was watching a series of choices with no particular through line. There wasn't any compelling reason why he had made those particular choices.

► *How do you think Carl could take care of this problem?*

Whenever Carl's work would take on this choppy quality, I knew that he hadn't made a strong enough decision of intent.

He said to me, "I thought if I made strong choices, intent wasn't such a big deal." To which I replied, "Well, Carl, it is a big deal! Your intent is what you want, it is the reason you have made those choices to begin with! *How can you know how you're going to get something before you know what it is you want to get?*"

Without intent, the choices come across as a random list of characteristics. With a strong intent, those same choices become a compelling and resonant picture of how you would go about getting what you want.

▶ *In short, intent gives your choices meaning.*

Carl finally realized the importance of identifying a strong intent and took the time in his preparation to dig deep and discover what he wanted in the piece. As a result, the choppy, start/stop quality in his work disappeared and his readings really started to flow. He found that a strong intent provided him with the through line that his work so badly needed.

In his first six auditions since taking class, Carl got five callbacks and booked two of the jobs. Working with focus and resolve on intent brought the consistency and strength he needed to be at his best every time.

▶Case Study #6: Stacey

STACEY WAS RELATIVELY NEW to acting when she joined my class. She was absolutely determined to be the best actress she could be and win any and every job she had the opportunity to audition for. She was also one of the funniest and most dynamic people I have ever taught.

She took to the technique as if she had been doing it all of her life and had very few problems until we got to adjustments.

When she delivered her adjusted reading, one of two things would happen: she would let the adjustment take over the entire piece, or she would rush and become tentative.

▶*How would you help Stacey solve her problems with adjustments?*

Stacey's predicament with this part of the audition process is one that affects many actors.

When she would get an adjustment, her brain would immediately switch over to "crowd pleasing" mode. She would panic and feel rushed. She told me that she would start to think about getting the adjustment "right" no matter what! *It was as if she saw the adjustment as a correction of her initial work, instead of a validation of how strong the work was to begin with.* So, she would either push too hard to prove she could "do it right," or hold back in case she was "doing it wrong."

When she realized that getting an adjustment was a good thing—and took that very important moment to breathe—she started to relax and take care of herself. She would silently pat herself on the back, see the casting director as someone who was on her side, and ask questions if she had them. She now had the confidence to ask for the time she needed to incorporate the adjustment, so that it wouldn't take over the entire piece. Finally, when she started the adjusted reading, she took her time, remembered her technique and listened.

Once Stacey was able to see that adjustments were a positive statement about her work, she began to behave in a positive manner in the room—not pushing, not getting anxious, simply adjusting. This shift in perception freed her to be at her best all the way through her auditions. She obtained a top-tier agent shortly after taking class and is currently working consistently in television, films and commercials.

▶Part Three

AUDITION AND THE LIFE OF THE ACTOR

▶Positive Anxiety

THOSE ARE TWO WORDS you don't often see together! But there is such a thing and it is an important part of the learning process.

When you are learning a new technique, you are also leaving behind an old way of working that has been part of you for some time. Before you get to a place of comfort and relative security with your new technique, you will probably experience a feeling similar to jumping out of a plane and not being sure if the parachute will open.

This is the in-between place where your feet are not planted solidly on either the old or the new patch of ground. Even though it may not feel like it, this is a wonderful place to be. If you are not rooted in any one way of doing things, you become an open valve for new information and ways of creating.

There are many people who can't bear the feelings of insecurity that are brought up by being on this middle ground. These people are the ones that go running back to their old ways. They know that those ways don't work, but they would rather stay stuck in what is familiar than feel that they are "up in the air."

▶ *Then there are others who realize that "up in the air" is where the answers are!*

They will stay with the process because they know that a feeling of anxiousness precedes all good change. They are able to see this anxiousness as a sign of moving toward a better, truer way of working.

When you can look at the anxiety in this light, it no longer makes you anxious, but excited. You know you are on your way to something that will serve you better. Any thoughts of going backwards disappear and are replaced by a willingness to move through the process toward a technique that is compelling, true and effective for you.

▶Honesty

There is only one goal in an audition: *to tell the truth*. It is not to do what you think the casting director wants to see or to hide behind a complicated technique or to put on a show. It is to tell the truth about yourself and to let them see what it is that you and only you have to give to the role.

The role you are auditioning for is a person. So are you. What qualities of yours are you going to add to the words on the page? How do you define this person? These questions must be answered unguardedly and honestly in order for the people in the room to see what is special about you and what is yours to offer.

As adults, we are well armored. We all have walls that we have put in front of us to guard against hurt and rejection. We've all heard "no" when we were desperate to hear "yes," and have been wounded by the experience.

The walls of defensiveness, aggression, arrogance and cockiness are not who you are; they are what you do to hide who you are. They are the armor and it must be stripped off. The qualities that lie beneath the armor—vulnerability, compassion, love, hurt, playfulness, humor, edginess, anger, etc.—are what need to be seen. They are what will get you noticed. They are what will get you jobs.

Growing up is the process of being brave enough to know that the armor only gets in the way of a happy and fully experienced life. *It is realizing that armor is not safe as much as it is suffocating. It is not protecting you as much as it is hiding you.*

▶ *Auditioning requires the same outlook.*

I have had actors say to me that this type of honesty is too difficult, too exposing. They tell me that opening themselves up, and being truthful to the degree that they need to in order to get work, is too trying, too painful. I can certainly relate to how hard it can be to break the walls down. But down they must come if you are to have access to the qualities that truly define you. Down they must come if you are to achieve the level of honesty in your auditions that will start you on your way to success.

This process of auditioning is not about trying to be someone you are not. It is expressing who you already are, your wisdom, vitality, greatness, and, yes, your wounds and your scars. All of these are your tools. Use them to tell the truth.

▶Risk

RISK IS AN ESSENTIAL COMPONENT of a rich, full life. It is also essential to interesting and compelling acting and auditions. Risk represents a willingness to grow and to expand your horizons, and it is to be applauded. Being open to uncertainty is what makes life exciting and what will make your work worth watching.

Playing it safe on the other hand only serves to make you listless and your work sluggish, washed out, and dull.

When you choose to play safe and not risk anything, everything quickly becomes stale. You become a passive, as opposed to an active, participant in your life. You let potentially wonderful and educational experiences and relationships slip away because you feel it is wiser to protect yourself than it is to risk the unknown.

▶ *Safety equals stagnation and it is not wise in the least.*

You may find a great deal of support in taking the safe road. This is because most other people are on that road and not only want some company, but are threatened by the idea of you transcending them.

These are the people who, when you were little, tried to stop you from going on the really cool rides at the amusement park. They said it was for your own good, you might get frightened, you might get nauseous, etc. Actually, what was going on was that they were scared and didn't want to be alone! They grow up to be the people who tell you, as an adult, that if you extend yourself personally or professionally you may get hurt again. Well, guess what? You are going to get hurt now and then and so will they. At least you will get to enjoy the ride.

If you don't take your life for a good ride and take the risks that make being alive so exciting, you will dry up and so will your work.

Your auditions are an extension of you and your life. If you choose the safe path in life, the stagnation that safety breeds will reflect in the choices you make in your work. The two are inexorably linked. The choices you make can only be as interesting, rich and full as your experience of life.

▶Simplicity

IN ORDER FOR the casting people to be able to see who you are in an audition, you must guard against embellishing your reading. If you have identified an intent that is compelling to you and drives you through the piece, if your choices are clear and honest and if the relationship(s) in the piece have been defined and are meaningful to you, all you need to do is open your ears and listen and open your mouth and speak.

Many actors fall into the trap of overselling themselves, or putting on a show in order to make what they think will be a good impression. However, if you have done the work discussed above, there is no need to try to be special. There is nothing to sell. The decisions you have made will naturally and truthfully set you apart from the rest. *They are special because they are yours.*

If you trust that this is the case, you will relax, the walls will come down, and the people watching you will be able to see exactly what you have to offer. If you do not trust this you will feel the need to add to the choices (ie, cry, laugh hysterically, yell, scream, etc.). You will then disconnect from yourself and all you will show is the effort you are making to elicit a positive response to your "work." These demonstrations of supposed skills will ultimately be seen for what they are: a fearful and effort-laden attempt to impress. The lack of trust and confidence that you will have shown by your willingness to sell yourself out will leave the strongest impression in the room—a room by the way that you will almost certainly not see the inside of again.

There is nothing as tedious as someone trying to be interesting. There is nothing as interesting as a person who has the strength and trust to know he doesn't have to try.

> ▶ *There is great power and confidence in simplicity.*
> *Don't give that power away.*

▶Blind Date

T HE DYNAMIC of an audition is not that much different from
that of a blind date.

Have you ever had a truly awful blind date? Come on, be honest, you know what I'm talking about! You're excited and curious.
You really want to get to know this potential new love interest.
You can't wait!

And then it happens. You spend an entire evening enduring the
posturing, bragging and dullness of a person you now can't wait
to get away from. You get home, call the person who set you up,
and are about to give them a piece of your mind when they ask
you, "Well, what were they like?" Suddenly it occurs to you that
you have no idea what they were like. All you saw was the insecurity of someone who so desperately didn't want to be rejected.
You can't answer the question because the date gave you nothing
but attitudes designed to please. Even though you just spent 4
hours with them you know nothing about how they feel, what has
meaning for them, or how they look at the world.

Then there is the good date—a little less common than the one
noted above, but so wonderful when it happens. The other person is open and honest. They have no concerns about being
rejected so they are confident, relaxed and available. You realize
that you too are being open, feeling at ease, and fun. When the
evening is over you can't wait to call your friend and thank them.

An audition is not that much different. You are walking into a situation with a total stranger, hoping that when it is over they will have a good idea of who you are, what your particular point of view is, and how you feel.

A bad audition contains all of the elements of the bad blind date. You walk into the room defensively. Your choices are not *your* choices, they're crowd-pleasing attitudes. You are not willing to put yourself on the line and show who you are for fear of being rejected. Your audition is full of posturing, walls are up in front of you with no windows to look through.

▶ *A good audition, like a good blind date, provides the person or people watching you with vital information about what makes you tick.*

You must be willing, through the decisions that you have made, to let the people get to know you. You must be open and honest, unafraid of rejection, bold, relaxed, and fun to be with. If you are, they will behave like a good date should: they will be attentive, responsive and supportive. Most importantly, they will not forget to call!

▶The Zone

WHEN ATHLETES ARE ASKED what it means to be "in the zone," the one common thread in their responses is that in the zone there is no doubt and no second-guessing. Most importantly of all, *there is no thinking.* Every decision is contained in their bodies and is blissfully automatic.

They are relaxed and powerful, secure in the knowledge that all of their training and preparation will be there to support them.

The same holds true for an audition. The trust you need to have in your preparation should be as strong as the trust the athlete has in his training.

Your preparation has been thorough and complete. All of the decisions that you have made are yours to make. Your intent, your relationships, your choices are a part of you. They are yours and, as such, don't need to be kept track of or thought about in the room. They will be there because you will be there.

Your work is done before the audition. That is why it is called preparation! By the time you open the door to the audition room, you have nothing left to do but open your mouth, open your ears, and blow away the people in the room with the power of your presence.

That is "the zone" that you as an actor should be aspiring to, the place where there is no need for thought, process or work. It is the place where you are able to flow easily and naturally, where you have the trust and the confidence to let all doing go and simply be.

> ▶ *It is the place where you show us purely and effortlessly who you are.*

►True Connection: The Importance of Listening

T HE WORDS OF THE PIECE that you are reading and the decisions that you have made about them are some of the tools
you have to express yourself in the audition. However, to rely on
the words as the sole way of showing who you are is extremely
limiting. Words by themselves are only going to show us a small
part of what you have to offer.

Have you ever had the experience of trying to tell someone
something that is very important to you and you say, "I just can't
find the words to describe it?" That's because the intensity and
depth of the experience transcend the limits of the language.

Language *is* limited. It is one tool of communication. It is by
no means the only way you have of communicating.

Your other tools of communication in the audition are *listening
and reacting*. They will allow you to express what can't be expressed
through words alone.

How you listen to and react to the person you are reading with
will tell them just as much, if not more, about you than the words
alone ever could. Listening with real attention and intensity takes
away the temptation to push or oversell the dialogue. You relax
when you are speaking because you know that you will be convey-
ing the decisions of intent, relationship and choices through your
listening and your reactions as well as through your reading. You

become secure in the knowledge that they are learning about you every second of your audition.

Listening is the purest way for you to show your point of view. The purity comes from the fact that there are no words in the way. The silences are you at your most honest. *Listening is your opportunity to show who you are without the encumbrance of the words.*

Silence and reaction represent a higher octave of expression than speaking. In music, the moment between one moment of sound and the next moment of sound is called the middle note. The middle note is what makes one orchestra's version of a symphony unique. It is why you can hear the same piece of music played by a hundred different orchestras, and think that some are wonderful and involving while others leave you cold. The actual notes being played are exactly the same; it is how the moments in between the notes are filled that either draws you in or pushes you away. The same is true for an audition. The words that everyone is reading are the same. The moments of silence and reaction in between the words give the piece its depth and make it unique to you.

Words can often create distance because they have less to do with feeling than they do with ideas. Your job in the audition is not to instruct or to explain to us why we should feel a certain way. Your job is to show us what you want us to feel, and further, what you can make an audience feel. You do this through the strength of your intent, the personal connection to your relationship, the truth of your choices, and the acute, passionate, honesty of your listening.

▶ *Words may be limited in their ability to express the truth, but the good news is—you are not limited to just the words.*

▶Pure Presence:
The Charismatic Actor

CHARISMA is a quality that we assign to certain actors who are so compelling and fascinating to watch that we can't put our finger on exactly what makes them so arresting. It seems like magic.

In one of my classes recently, a student asked if charisma is something that can be learned or if it is a quality that some people are just born with. Before I could answer, I had to think long and hard about how to define this most mysterious of qualities.

I believe that charisma is the result of complete attention to another person. Someone we call charismatic is able to be totally engrossed in the person they are with. All of their energy flows in the direction of the other person—they are 100% present.

They are able to be involved to such a high degree that the person being spoken to sees only their best qualities reflected back to them in the eyes of this charismatic individual—they feel that who they are and what they have to say is actually worthy of all of this undivided attention.

Think of how rarely we meet someone who is that unselfishly involved. Most people have only about half of their attention on the person they are with.

See if this sounds familiar: You are speaking to someone, you see the person looking at you—and yet you have the unsettling feeling that they are making out their grocery list as you are spilling your guts.

Compare that to the person described above and ask yourself who you want to spend more time with.

So can charisma be learned? If we operate under the premise that charisma is pure outwardly focused attention to another, I believe that it can be learned. But more importantly, it must be cultivated. That will take a good deal of vigilance on your part. You need to make sure in every encounter you have that your attention and focus are entirely on the other person—with no judgment or thoughts of what the outcome of the exchange will be.

Now, let's apply this concept to acting and more specifically to the audition process.

In order to be looked upon as an actor who has true charisma, your mind has to be clear of anything that will get in between you and the other person in the room. You need to have the degree of confidence in your technique and preparation that will allow you not to think about what you are doing, but to just let it happen.

If you have any doubts about the decisions that you have made for the piece, you will be distracted by those doubts during the audition. If you have overworked the piece, you will be anticipating your next line instead of being completely present with each line as it comes. Remember, charisma comes from your attention to and focus on the other person.

Anything that distracts you from giving that degree of attention needs to be addressed and corrected.

Thought and anticipation can now be seen as the enemy of charisma. They create distance from the other person by putting the focus on you instead of on them. When you are willing to let go of thinking and anticipating, when you have prepared the material so that these processes are unnecessary, all of that energy can be spent listening to and taking in the other person. You will be bridging the distance between yourself and the person instead of widening it.

▶ *Charisma is the ability to have your mind utterly clear and uncluttered.*

Only then can you be completely present. Yes, it can be learned. It may not be easy, but it's a very noble goal to aim for, and believe me, the rewards will be far greater than you could imagine.

You will now possess that magic quality that others, whether they can define it or not, can't get enough of, and can't deny.

After all, who wouldn't want to hire an actor who is so assured and so strong in themselves that they can be completely available to others? Many would call that person a star.

▶Being and Doing

THE WALLACE AUDITION TECHNIQUE was designed to give you the tools you need to be in the room exactly as you want to be. However, none of this technique will work until you provide the most important element: trust.

Trust comes from the knowledge that the work you have done preparing the piece is honest, connected, and technically sound.

If you believe that this is the case, you can let all of your work go. You can simply "be" in the audition, secure that your preparation will be there to support you.

Trusting that simply "being" will be enough is probably the biggest mental hurdle in this process. This is why most actors wind up "doing" too much. They sell too hard, push too much, and leave nothing but work and effort in their wake.

Given the way that most of us were brought up to live in the world, it is no wonder that it's so hard for us to believe that just being ourselves is enough.

It starts from the first time you were told that you were a good kid only when you did something. For example, you were told that you were good if you ate all your dinner. You were good if you cleaned your room. You were good if you got decent grades in school, and on and on.

Very few of us were told that we were good—period. The implication was that just being ourselves wasn't enough. We had to do something specific to earn praise. This is a pattern that gets set in our minds from a very early age and is reinforced throughout our lives. We continually jump through hoops. We hope that if we do enough, someone will notice us, praise us, and tell us that we're worthwhile. Maybe they'll even tell us that we're good enough to be hired.

Auditioning and acting for the camera, however, are not about doing. The "doing" is your preparation, and as we've talked about, it should be finished by the time the actual audition starts. It should free you to just "be."

Doing hides who you are. It creates a wall of effort between you and the people watching you—*and no meaningful connection can be made through a wall.*

If you believe that your preparation will support you and that your decisions are actually a part of you, then you will have the confidence to simply be. You will know that in every moment you are effortlessly showing who you are and the genuine life that you have to bring to the words on the page. You will be connecting in the unique and personal way that leads to work.

In order to expand yourself as a person and as an actor, it may be necessary to examine and perhaps reverse certain ideas and teachings from your past. This is an important part of growing up: clearing out the cobwebs every once in a while and making space for new ideas and ways of doing things.

▶ *Learning and perfecting a technique that allows you the freedom to let go and just **be** is a good start!*

►Experience versus Intellect

THE INTELLECT presents one of the biggest challenges to living a full and richly experienced life. We depend on our minds to get us through life much more than we depend on our instincts.

This overdependence on the intellect is also what keeps actors from doing the sort of personal and unique work that affects the viewer on a visceral level.

Many people hold dear to certain beliefs about the power of the intellect:

► There is a logical explanation for everything.

► Life can be intellectualized and figured out.

► Thinking and reasoning are the paths to happiness and security.

The problem with these beliefs is that they completely fly in the face of how life works. They presume that life somehow stops and allows us the time and distance to put it in order.

Life never stops. It is continually happening around us and to us. Your only real job is to experience it, to really live it.

Your job is not to manage life—it is too unwieldy. It is not to make life neat—it is too messy. It is not to make sense of life—it rarely holds up to logic. And forget about trying to make life small and safe. It is just way too big.

You must live and experience your life fully and passionately no matter how hard it may be. Live it when it is happy, joyful, exciting and ecstatic, and don't hide under the covers when it is sad, boring, bewildering, or heartbreaking.

The depth and honesty with which you live your life will be reflected in your work as an actor. Your job is to take in all that life has to offer and to give it back to an audience through your eyes and your heart.

One of the most common regrets that people have as they get older is that they have spent too much time trying to make sense out of their lives and not enough time actually living their lives. They finally realize that the idea that life can be figured out, reasoned, or organized is an illusion and that trying to do so has been a waste of time.

Many of these people will tell you that during their lives they have had friends who seemed to just drift through life. When asked what they planned to do with their lives, these friends would say, "I'm just going with the flow." They would judge these friends as being lazy and shiftless.

As they got older, however, they realized that these "go with the flow" people had it right all along! They innately knew that the "flow" was all there was, and that any attempts to find logic in the flow of life were pointless. They accepted and found joy in the pure experience of living.

This leads us back to you as an actor. If you go about preparing an audition piece just by using your logical mind, the piece will end up having very little life.

> ▸ *Your work must be about your experience of life,*
> *not your academic opinion of life.*

The audition technique that we work on exists to free you to share what is unique in your experience, what informs your existence. That is what will make you stand out. That is what will make you compelling and undeniable. That is what will get you the job.

Acting, whether performance or audition, is simply a distilled expression of your particular humanity. That expression has to come purely from your experience and it needs to be specific to you. The fact that your experience is fueling the expression will make your work tangibly compelling, accessible to all who see it, and immediately recognizable as the truth.

▶Image versus Reality: Staying True to the Real You

Too many actors get caught up in worrying about other people's perceptions of who they are. They believe that if they behave in a way that pleases others, all will be well: they will be loved, popular, and, as actors, a shoe-in to ace their auditions and book their jobs.

These people spend a lot of time working to shape their personalities to fit the opinions and desires of others. In this way, they feel that they can create and put forth an image that will be pleasing and acceptable. An image, however, is not real. It is a compilation of traits that a person feels will gain approval from others, a stitching together of what they feel they should be and how they should behave. What they are really doing is creating a monster, and a boring one at that!

This tendency doesn't occur by accident. Acting is a business that has no concrete formula for success. You will find that if you ask 50 working actors how they got where they are you'd get 50 different answers.

You will also find, if you haven't already, that everyone has an opinion on what you need to be or do in order to succeed. (Most of these people, by the way, will be the ones that aren't working.) As an actor, you need to have a filter through which to run all of this "advice"—ask yourself if what you are hearing is right for you. Without this filter, you are too vulnerable to other people's views of who you should be or what you should be doing. That is when the real you can begin to disappear in favor of the image formed by what other people think is best.

If you feel it is necessary to create an image in place of being yourself, you are giving too much credibility to other people's opinion of you.

▶ *You cannot be yourself and an image of yourself at the same time.*

It is one or the other. You are you, or you are a copy of you; authentic, or fraudulent. This is the essential choice every actor who wants to work and wants to achieve greatness must make.

When you are focused on projecting an image, you also become your own worst critic. Qualities that are truly yours are judged and eliminated by the part of you that believes your image is the key to success. Many of the strongest, most compelling parts of your personality are dismissed from your behavior and edited out of your work. The insecurity and weakness that make hiding behind a self-image necessary in the first place will also ensure that nothing that contradicts that image will find its way in.

You and your work will become as small as the image that you have created.

Images, copies and concepts don't get work. They are simply a small, scared projection of what you hope will be acceptable to others. In order to make your work truly come alive and be a strong representation of you and what you have to offer, you need access to all of you, not just parts of you. You must be willing to explore and share all of your qualities without judgment, fear, or any imagined need for approval.

▶Playing It Big

I WAS GIVING A TALK to a group of actors a few years ago. Among the topics I was discussing was how important it is for actors to be connected to the strongest aspects of their personalities in auditions.

During the question and answer period, an actor stood up and asked me, "So many actors have such big personalities. I have always lived a pretty sheltered life and I like it that way. I don't know how to compete with actors who have lived so much more than I have—they seem bigger than life. What can I do about this?"

My immediate response was, "It is not possible for anyone to be bigger than life. Life is everything that is happening to everyone everywhere; no one can be bigger than that. What you have just told me is how small you believe your life is."

I asked him how he was doing in his auditions. He told me that he felt nervous and intimidated and that he didn't commit to his choices.

None of that surprised me. The fact that he felt that everyone else was "bigger" was causing him to back off in his auditions. His commitment was weak because he felt small before he even walked into the room.

There are many people, like this actor, who are simply overwhelmed by how big life truly is. They spend much time and energy making their lives small in an effort to create an illusion of safety.

I'm sure you know some of these people. When asked what they think life is about, they will reply with something like, "My life is about my home, my job and my car." And they stop there. They refuse to acknowledge that there is so much life going on outside of their small parameters. They have put on blinders in order to feel "in control."

There is only one problem with this way of "living:" it doesn't work. Life doesn't recognize people's arbitrary boundaries. It can't be kept out.

As actors, it is essential to observe and experience all of life, and to expand and eventually dissolve the walls that can keep you small and uninvolved.

> ▶ *The roles that you are auditioning for will only have*
> *as much life as you have to bring to them.*

If you commit to enthusiastically experiencing all that life has to offer, your work will automatically have the energy and passion of a life fully lived.

Conversely, if you spend all of your time trying to keep life out, your range of possibilities will shrink to fit the smallness of your life.

It may be impossible to be *bigger* than life, but you can be *as big as life*. If you are, the life in your work will be unique, powerful and undeniable. Life is big. Don't run from it—show up for it. It will then show up for you in your work.

▶I Quit—
The Quest for Self-Approval

THERE IS A STRENGTH, a confidence, a presence connected to the actors casting directors love to see in auditions. These are the actors who walk into the room bringing definite answers about who the character is as they see it. They are excited for the casting director to see all of their rich and dynamic choices. They are the actors who don't need anything from anyone. They are bringing the whole party with them.

These actors, as we've discussed, are in the minority. Most actors walk into an audition not bringing much of anything. Their work is tentative and weak. They aren't bringing answers, they are bringing questions. They seem to need something from other people in order to feel good about themselves and their work.

What they are looking for is approval. They need to be shown that it is okay to be themselves, that their choices are "right," before they are willing to let go and just be.

The actors that casting directors and producers love, on the other hand, have given themselves permission to let go and be. They have complete control over themselves and their auditions.

What can you do to be one of the actors people love and avoid the neediness of the actors who aren't loved?

Since what you are bringing to your auditions is a reflection of who you are, it may be a good idea to take a look at how you are functioning in the world—specifically, how important other people's opinions are to you and how necessary their approval may be for you to feel good about yourself.

> ▶ *The belief that you need to be approved of by anyone*
> *but yourself is simply false.*

It is a game. A game created by people who have so little self-esteem and confidence that the only way they can feel any power and control is to convince you that their opinion matters. They need your insecurity to validate their existence.

This is a horrible and demeaning dynamic and if you start to really believe these people, they can sap your strength and create a sense of dependency that will drain all of your power.

The good news is if you have your eyes open and see these people for who they really are from the start, you won't get trapped.

> ▶ *Remember, it is a game—*
> *one that you can win by simply not playing.*

The next time you find yourself seeking approval outside of yourself, and/or you are in contact with someone who is trying to convince you that their approval of you is essential, simply say to yourself: "I QUIT!"

"I will not smile and laugh when I am unhappy so that you will feel comfortable and approve of my behavior—I QUIT!"

"I will not nod my head in agreement every time you open your mouth and keep my own thoughts to myself so that you will feel validated—I QUIT!"

"I will not tolerate the lie that your approval of my thoughts and behavior are essential to my existence—I QUIT!"

"I will not try to look like the models on the 20 billboards I pass on my way to work everyday. I don't need the advertising industry telling me that I need those products so I will be adored. I also know that next month there will be twenty new billboards telling me I need 20 new products and that if I use those products, maybe then I will be approved of—I QUIT!"

"I quit" doesn't mean "I give up"—just the opposite. When you quit the game of approval-seeking and people-pleasing you get all of your own power back. You can now focus on being the person that you want to be.

The tone of your auditions will also shift—big time! You will no longer walk into the room seeking approval. You will have approved of yourself and the decisions that you have made before you walk into the room. You will be the strong, confident actor that they want to hire!

▶Part Four

DO'S AND DON'TS:
HOW TO BE AT YOUR BEST
DURING EACH STEP OF THE AUDITION

THE READING is only one part of the audition process. The moments before and after the reading are of equal importance and need to be handled strongly and professionally.

▶ The Waiting Room

There are actors who will insist on telling you how great they are, how well their careers are going, how right they are for the role and other similar nonsense.

> ▶ **DON'T...** *let other actors in the waiting room psych you out.*

> ▶ **DO...** *find a spot where you can be quiet and collect yourself.*

Go outside, down the hall or even to the restroom. If none of that is possible, tell the person who is chattering at you that you'd like to have a few quiet moments to focus. If they're professional they will respect your request. If they're not professional and continue talking, just move away from them. *You are not responsible for making their waiting time enjoyable.*

▶ Walking into the Room

I used to work with a casting director who would watch actors very closely as they entered the room. She claimed that she could tell in the first two steps they took whether they were going to deliver a strong and connected reading or not. She was always right!

How you enter a room sets the tone for everything that will follow.

▶ **DON'T...** *rush into the room with your head down. This is the first impression that the casting director will have of you.* ***You can't start a positive audition experience from a negative stance.***

▶ **DO...** *walk in confidently with your head up. Not only is it our first impression of you, it is also your first opportunity to see the room you will be reading in and the people you will be reading for. Take note of the layout. Where are the casting director and/or producers? See if there is a camera and where it is placed. Take a good look at the space you will be reading in. Chances are the room will be smaller than you imagined. Many times it is the casting director's office. The faster you take in the parameters of the room, the more comfortable you will be in the space when it is time for your reading.*

▶ **DON'T...** *make anxious, unfocused chitchat.*

▶ **DO...** *make eye contact. Say hello and how are you. If the opportunity presents itself, shake hands firmly. Take the temperature of the room. If the casting director/ producers are in a talkative mood, take advantage of it and use the time to have fun and loosen up. If they are all business, then you should be too.*

▶ Setting Up the Room

In order to give the best possible audition, you need to make sure that there is no doubt about the logistics of the room. For example, if you are unsure about who you are going to be reading with, or if you're not certain if they want you reading directly into the camera—ask! It's your audition and your room, so take charge of it.

A student of mine tells a story that points up the importance of setting the room up properly. This is a rather extreme example but it certainly makes the point. The student had her first big network test at a major studio. When she walked into the room, which would normally fit about 10 people comfortably, she saw almost 40 people sitting all over the room, on chairs, on the floor, behind the space where she would be reading, behind the camera. Every inch of the room was covered with producers, studio executives, network executives, and casting executives. Instead of going into panic mode, she walked in, looked around the room and said in as friendly and fun a way as she could, "Okay, which people here can actually hire me for this job?" At which point, two of the network executives and the director raised their hands! She asked them if they would please move and stand next to the reader, who was behind the camera. And guess what? They did! The people in the room thought it was so great that she had the guts to set the room up to her advantage that even before her actual reading they had decided that she had the part. They knew that this was an actress who would be able to deliver her best no matter what the circumstances, and that gave them all the confidence they needed to hire her.

▶ **DON'T...** *fidget around waiting to be told where to go.*

▶ **DO...** *ask where they would like you to be and take your space in the room.*

▶ **DON'T...** *leave any doubt about where your reading should be directed, especially if you are being taped.*

▶ **DO...** *ask where they would like your reading to be focused. If you are being taped, make sure you know whether they would prefer you to read to the person running the camera or directly to the camera.*

▶ The Moment Before

This is your last opportunity before the reading to compose your-self and to solidify your control of the room.

> ▶ **DON'T...** *start until you are absolutely ready.*

> ▶ **DO...** *tell the casting director that you would like to take a moment. In that moment, take a deep breath and remind yourself of what your intent and relation-ship are. This will ensure that you will be focused and strong from the very beginning of the reading.*

► The Reading

You've owned the room up until this point. Now it is time to hit it out of the park.

If you have worked the technique through, as laid out in Chapters 1-6, you will have identified a compelling intent and a meaningful relationship. You will have made strong and connected choices that are clear and will be cleanly delivered.

> ► **DON'T...** *rush through the reading as if it was a race to the finish line.*

> ► **DO...** *take your time. Trust that the work you have done will support you, then let it go. All of the decisions that you have made deserve to be seen in exactly the way you want them seen.*
>
> ***Read the piece your way and at your pace.***
>
> *If the reader is flat or monotone in their delivery, just keep listening and remember the relationship that you have established. This will keep the energy of the reading up where it needs to be and you won't get dragged down into their monotonous rhythm. Stay relaxed, stay calm, and make each moment count. And finally, know that the confidence that you are showing in yourself and your decisions will be shared by the people watching you.*

▶ The Moment After

So far, you have entered and set the room up strongly and read with confidence and commitment. Now, you must finish the audition leaving no doubt in the people's minds that they have just seen a real professional.

▶ **DON'T...** *assume that just because the reading is over that the audition is over. You are still being watched and considered, so don't all of a sudden "go weak" (ie, look down at the floor or away from the casting director with the attitude of, "was that okay?").*

▶ **DO...** *hold the eyes of the casting director or reader after you have finished. If there is a pause say, "Is there anything else you'd like to see?" This is a very positive statement. It tells them that you can handle any changes that they come up with. If they want to see more, go through the steps outlined in the chapter on adjustments. Stay strong and connected to them. When you know that you are definitely finished, be polite and professional. Thank them for seeing you and tell them that you look forward to seeing them again soon.*

▶ **DON'T...** *say, "So, when are callbacks?" This sounds arrogant and cocky and makes everyone in the room uncomfortable. It will end your audition on a sour note and erase any good work you did in the reading.*

▶ The Drive Home

Believe it or not you're still not finished with your audition. It is now time to have a look back at what just happened and, finally, let it go.

▶ **DON'T...** *replay the audition a thousand times in your head looking for reasons to beat yourself up.*

▶ **DO...** *take an objective look at the entire process, from being in the waiting room through walking out of the door. See yourself going through each step and identify what went well. If any part of the audition wasn't exactly as you wanted it to be, go through your technique and find the step(s) that could have been stronger.*

▶ **DON'T...** *carry negative baggage from one audition to the next.*

▶ **DO...** *use each audition as a learning experience. Make the changes in your head that would have improved the audition you just had, and commit to strengthening that part of your process. Write the changes down in a place where you will see them before you prepare your next audition. Now, let it go. You have learned what you needed from the experience and are ready to move on to the next.*

►Conclusion

B Y READING THIS BOOK, you have shown a great deal of commitment to yourself and your career. You have dedicated this time to learning and perfecting the skills you need to get the job. Congratulations!

You now have the knowledge that will allow you to walk into any audition and show the casting directors and producers the possibilities that are unique to you in a clear, confident and powerful way. You also have the technical ability that will give to you the freedom to listen and be present in the room.

Your auditions will have the perfect balance of dynamic reading and magnetic attentiveness. Every person who sees you will be compelled to pay full attention and will be left wanting more.

You are also on your way to being stronger and more secure in who you are, no longer needing or wanting the approval of others.

Finally, I hope you are realizing that your greatness lies within, and that you are able to fully express it with the help of what you have learned from this book.

If so, it won't be long before that greatness is up on the screen for all the world to see.

I wish that degree of success for each and every one of you.

Now, get to work!

▶About the Author

THE WALLACE AUDITION TECHNIQUE was created by 20-year industry professional Craig Wallace.

Craig has been a development executive, producer, head of talent development, and talent agent.

As a development executive at United Artists Craig read thousands of motion picture and television scripts. From this experience came his ability to teach actors how to break down scripts and sides quickly and creatively.

During his tenure as a casting executive and producer, he auditioned hundreds of actors. Craig saw firsthand why certain actors consistently booked the jobs and why others did not.

While working at one of the top talent agencies in Los Angeles, he saw how important it was for actors to have a strong and reliable technique that would guide them through the entire audition process. Using all of this experience, Craig worked with other casting directors, agents and producers to develop The Wallace Audition Technique.

Since then, hundreds of actors have taken The Wallace Audition Technique classes and many have gone on to highly successful careers in television, films and commercials.

Craig has given numerous lectures at universities, bookstores, and many actors' and artists' organizations.

He has also coached people from a wide variety of professions on how to improve their public speaking and presentation skills.

▶For more information on classes and workshops please visit:

www.wallaceauditiontechnique.com